THE ESSENTIAL POINTS
OF PRACTICE

A MANUAL OF BASIC INSTRUCTIONS
ON THOROUGH CUT
BY ZHECHEN GYALTSHAB

TONY DUFF
PADMA KARPO TRANSLATION COMMITTEE

This text is secret and should not be shown to those who
have not had the necessary introduction and instructions of
the Thorough Cut system of Dzogchen meditation. If you
have not had the necessary instructions, reading this text can
be harmful to your spiritual health! Seal. Seal. Seal.

First edition, November 2008
ISBN: 978-9937-9031-5-8

Janson typeface with diacritical marks and
Tibetan Classic typeface
Designed and created by Tony Duff
Tibetan Computer Company
http://www.tibet.dk/tcc

Produced, Printed, and Published by
Padma Karpo Translation Committee
P.O. Box 4957
Kathmandu
NEPAL

Web-site and e-mail contact through:
http://www.tibet.dk/pktc
or search Padma Karpo Translation Committee on the web.

CONTENTS

INTRODUCTION

This is a short but very clear text on the essential points of the practice of the Great Completion's Thorough Cut[1]. It was written by Zhechen Gyaltshab Rinpoche, of Zhechen Monastery, for one of his disciples, as noted in the colophon. The Zhechen Gyaltshab's have always been known as master scholars and highly accomplished practitioners of the Great Completion teaching. The translation is intended for those people who have the instructions for the

Zhechen Gyaltshab

practice. Rather than writing a long introduction to explain the flow of the text, I have written very extensive footnotes and included a glossary to make the text as accessible as possible and to clarify points that are might not otherwise be clear.

---

[1] Tib. khregs chod. Thregcho. See the glossary for more.

Our Supports for Study

I have been encouraged over the years by all of my teachers and gurus to pass on some of the knowledge I have accumulated in a lifetime dedicated to the study and practice, primarily through the Tibetan Buddhist tradition, of Buddhism. On the one hand they have encouraged me to teach. On the other hand, they are concerned that, while many general books on Buddhism have been and are being published, there are few books that present the actual texts of the tradition. They and many other, closely involved people have encouraged me to make and publish high quality translations of individual texts of the tradition.

In general, we have published a wide range of books that present the important literature of Tibetan Buddhism. In particular, the author of this book was one of the key figures in the transmission of the most profound Great Completion teachings in Tibet and we have published many of the important texts of that system, with each one carefully selected to inform about a particular aspect of that teaching. Other texts of ours which deal with the same subject as this one but which add their own, particular ornamentation are *The Feature of the Glorious, Expert King* by Patrul Rinpoche, *About the Three Lines* by Dodrupchen III, *Alchemy of Accomplishment* by Dudjom Jigdral Yeshe Dorje, *Hinting at Dzogchen* by Tony Duff, *Way of the Old Dogs* by Ju Mipham Namgyal, and so on.

All in all, you will find many books both for free and for sale on our web-site, all of them prepared to the highest level of quality. Many of our books are available not only on paper but as electronic editions that can be downloaded, and all of them are prepared to the highest level of quality. We encourage you to look at our web-site to see what we have; the address is on the copyright page at the front of this book. Major book sellers also carry our paper editions.

It has also been a project of ours to make tools that non-Tibetans and Tibetans alike could use for the study and translation of Tibetan texts. As part of that project, we prepare electronic editions of Tibetan texts in the Tibetan Text input office of the Padma Karpo Translation Committee and make them available to the world. Tibetan texts are often corrupt so we make a special point of carefully correcting our work before making it available through our web-site. Thus, our electronic texts are not careless productions like most Tibetan texts found on the web but are highly reliable editions that can be used by non-scholars and scholars alike. Moreover, many of the texts are free. The Tibetan text for this book is available for download as a free, electronic edition. It is also included at the back of the book as an aid to serious study.

Our electronic texts can be read, searched, and so on, using our Tibetan software. The software can be used to set up a reference library of these texts and then used to read and even research them quickly and easily. The software, called TibetD and TibetDoc, has many special features that make it useful not only for reading but also for understanding and even translating texts. One key feature is that you can highlight a Tibetan term in a text then look it up immediately in any of our electronic dictionaries. We suggest the highly acclaimed *Illuminator Tibetan-English Dictionary* as the best dictionary for the purpose. As with all of our publications, the software and electronic texts can be obtained from our web-site whose address is on the copyright page at the front of the book.

Health Warning

The text here is about a subject that is kept secret. Therefore, I have translated the text as it is, providing enough notes so that someone who does understand the meaning could understand the translation without mistake. However, I have deliberately not given any further explanation of or commentary to the meaning. Anyone who has had these teachings in person will be able to understand them or at least go to his teacher and ask for further explanation. Anyone who has heard these teachings in person from a qualified teacher, and especially who has had the introduction to the nature of mind[2] around which the teachings hinge, please use and enjoy the texts as you will! However, if you have not heard these teachings and if you have not had a proper introduction to the nature of your mind, you would be better off not reading this book but seeking out someone who could teach it to you. These days there are both non-Tibetans and Tibetans who can do that for you and who are available in many countries across our planet. In short, the contents of this book could be dangerous to your spiritual health if you are not ready for it, so exercise care.

---

[2] Introduction to the nature of mind is mostly mis-translated these days as "pointing out" instruction.

The principal lineage teachers of innermost Great Completion as it came into Tibet including Garab Dorje, the source of the teaching in general and the Three Lines teaching in particular. Garab Dorje above left, Manjushrimitra above right, Vimalamitra below left, Shri Singha below right of Padmasambhava in the centre. Mural on the wall of Dzogchen Monastery, Tibet, 2007. Photograph by the author.

These days, in the times of rampant globalization, these deep secrets have become very public. That is not necessarily a good thing. For example, I have many times in the last few years run into young men who are extremely confident of their understanding of the meaning of these profound systems but who just spout words that they have read in books. Unfortunately, they have read the books and know the words but have not contacted the inner meaning that the books are intended to be merely a pointer towards. The solidity of their minds is noticeable and it is not being helped by reading these things that they are not ready for and should not be reading.

My best wishes to all of you.
May you preserve the state!

Lama Tony Duff,
Swayambunath,
Nepal,
16th November 2008

THE ESSENTIAL POINTS OF PRACTICE

by Zhechen Gyaltshab

I prostrate to the second conqueror, the One of Samye, All-knowing Lord of Speech[3].

I will give some explanation of essential points of the practice that comes down from him[4].

To begin with, position your body on a comfortable seat with the key points of the Seven Dharmas of Vairochana held relaxed and comfortable. In particular, the eyes are a door of wisdom's shining forth[5] so, without focussing them on a

---

[3] This refers to Longchen Rabjam who was also known as a second conqueror and who referred to himself in his writings as "All-knowing One of Samye".

[4] The practice system of Great Completion with its two key practices of Thorough Cut and Direct Crossing. The first of the two is explained in this text.

[5] The eyes are a key place for making wisdom actually come, or shine, forth in mind.

support of some kind, you should tunnel your gaze[6] into the space directly ahead. The key point for speech is to let the wind of the breath come and go naturally but not through the nostrils, instead, it should be sent extremely gently through the mouth. There is a very great purpose behind each one of these points mentioned in this paragraph, so it is important not to under-rate them.

Then, as a preliminary, do the meditations of renunciation, disenchantment, and compassion-bodhichitta. Follow that by visualising a lotus and moon above the crown of your head with your root guru seated on it in his ordinary appearance[7]. Supplicate to the point of tears for the quick arousal in your mindstream of an outstanding realization of the profound path[8].

---

[6] Tib. ha re. To tunnel the gaze is to put the gaze ahead, staring into empty space, in a very focussed way. It is similar style of gaze to "piercingly" which is mentioned later on in the text.

[7] His appearance as you normally see it, rather than as a deity, etcetera.

[8] The profound path is the path here of Thorough Cut. An outstanding realization is a standard way of saying, in this system, one that is actually it. Realization in this system does not mean final realization but means that the innate nature of mind, which is called by many names, comes directly and nakedly to the practitioner. From that initial realization, one trains and trains so that final realization is obtained.

To say more about this point, mere talk, mere words are of no benefit—for the realization of Great Completion[9] to be born in your mindstream, there has to be a transmission of the blessings in the mindstream of a guru who has the lineage. That transmission is brought on by the disciple's devotion therefore it is important to make this alone the prime thing and to supplicate for this transmission over and again, bringing it on and bringing it on, practising and practising, planting a stake of supplication that will be undisturbed by thoughts of how good you have been with the practice so far. At the end, together with the key points of visualization that go with the four empowerments, mix the guru's mind and yours so that they are inseparable, then preserve[10], in freedom from grasping, the innate disposition of great bliss.

That is not talking about meditation done as the state of alaya which is devoid of every kind of thought process, a kind of oblivion, an indeterminate state. It is not meditation done in a state of alaya consciousness which is merely illuminative and knowing and has the factor of abiding and, similarly, it is not talking about meditation done as that state but with the blankness of the temporary experience of no-thought[11]. It is

---

[9] Realization has the same meaning as in the last footnote; it is the initial direct comprehension of the innate, not necessarily a high level of realization of it.

[10] See the glossary. This is a key term in Thorough Cut. The author gives a nice definition of it in the next paragraph.

[11] These different aspects of alaya are further clarified in the book *Differentiating Non-distraction and so on* by Tony Duff, published
(continued...)

also not talking about meditation which is just movement of discursive thoughts that happens when they apprehend an object and no movement when they do not[12]. Well then, what is it?[13] In the present of the previous discursive thought having ceased and the next one not having been born, self-

---

[11](...continued)
by Padma Karpo Translation Committee.

[12] Here, he gives four specific types of meditation that are not the Thorough Cut meditation being discussed in this text. There is a distinct difference in each case and you need to read carefully to see the differences. Note for instance that alaya and alaya consciousness are not the same thing. The first is a background, indeterminate state that is like nothingness. The second now has consciousness associated with it. The definition of consciousness is "illuminative and knowing" so those words here are being used to make a point that this is consciousness as opposed to the nothingness of alaya. The factor of abiding refers to the idea that the practitioner is simply abiding there in the consciousness itself. If you take that simple abiding in alaya consciousness a step further, you get the third type of meditation, which is that you are in alaya consciousness but without the clarity factor. That means that is a kind of non-knowing, which is described as blankness, "had de ba" in Tibetan. The fourth possibility is that you are simply sitting there, allowing thoughts to come and go, being aware of that, and not altering it. All of them are not Thorough Cut meditation for the simple reason that in all of them the practitioner has not, for whatever reason, cut through to the innate. Or, using the terminology of the previous paragraphs, the practitioner has not had the realization of the innate occur in the mindstream.

[13] So now he continues to state what the realization, which is the basis for the training, is like.

knowing free of the machinations of rational mind, simply seen without veil, unified luminosity-emptiness, a mind which is like space, shines forth[14]. It is the alpha purity of beyond-rational-mind Great Completion's Thorough Cut seen nakedly, in full transparency[15], dharmas exhausted[16]. So, having recognized it, there is the practice of gaining experience in it, which is that you put yourself nicely in it, with it left natural, and that is given the specific name "preservation"[17].

What is needed in any and every one of three contexts of view, meditation, and conduct, is to know this nakedly, with

---

[14] Tib. 'char ba. "To shine forth" has a very special meaning. It means that something comes forth in mind. The term is never used for something that appears to the physical senses even if the senses are involved; it always refers to the mind side of the equation. Furthermore, this word is special in that it is used to refer to something that comes forth in any mind, dualistic and non-dualistic. Here, it refers to the coming forth in non-dualistic mind that itself is wisdom.

[15] Tib. zang thal. This term has two meanings which go together, firstly of seeing directly and secondly of that view being unobscured. See transparency in the glossary for more.

[16] Dharmas in this case are the phenomena of dualistic mind. When you cut to this state of realization, dualistic dharmas necessarily have to end on the spot.

[17] Here is the definition of the key term of this system mentioned earlier, "preservation" and "to preserve".

a stripped-down awareness[18]. If it is not known, one person might show it to himself as something free from the three of birth, cessation, and dwelling[19] and another person might think, "It's like this", but doing any of those is like the nameless having gotten a name; in this cage of rational-mind-made mentation there is no chance that realization could happen. This dharmakaya of naked, empty rigpa beyond rational mind

---

[18] Tib. shes pa. Note that this is not a translation of "rigpa". These days it has become popular to translate "rigpa" with "awareness" but that is a gross error; see "rigpa" in the glossary for more. There is another term, the one here, which is the basic term for awareness. It is a generic term that is used for both dualistic and non-dualistic contexts. Consciousness (Tib. "rnam par shes pa") is the dualistic form of awareness. Rigpa, wisdom, and so on are non-dualistic forms of awareness. When you see "awareness" in this book, you should understand what has been explained here and look to see what context is being talked about. Currently, it is a non-dualistic awareness, one that has been stripped bare of its dualistic baggage that is being discussed.

[19] There is the practice of determining non-dualistic mind by the "parting into sides" practice, as it is called, of investigating where a moment of dualistic mind comes from, abides, and goes off to. It cannot be found, which is a way of getting to non-dualistic mind. However, if you sit there in your meditation going through these mental motions in order to show the non-dualistic rigpa to yourself, you are sitting there using concepts and putting them all over the actual rigpa. That is a less obvious mistake. A more obvious one is to use concepts simply to tell yourself "Oh, here it is, this is it", which again is to put concepts all over the actual rigpa.

cannot be pin-pointed within the mere generic images[20] produced by rational mind with its investigations and words for expressing something but the combination of the guru's blessings and one's own force of meditation can lead to its encounter using a simple, child-like process of thought in which exaggerations are cut internally[21] therefore it is important to have an unflagging, continuous perseverance at the meditation.

For beginners, there is the great danger connected with being excessively relaxed about the practice that the practice will turn into confusion. Therefore, beginners need to work at not being forgetful with watchful mindfulness[22]. It is an

---

[20] A generic image is a technical name for one type of conceptual structure involved with the operation of conceptual mind. A generic image is a concept that conceptual mind takes and uses instead of having a direct perception of the actual thing. For example, there is your concept of table, which is a complicated operation, one aspect of which is a generic image, and there is the actual direct sight of table, which has no concept attached to it. The whole process of rational, dualistic mind with its generic images can never get at something like rigpa which lies outside the reach of dualistic mind.

[21] Using rational mind to logically think something through and pin-point it is a process called "cutting exaggerations externally". The more profound style is for the exaggerations of dualistic mind to be cut internally. The latter approach requires no logical analysis but just a simple use of thought that is used then dropped as one cuts to the realization of innate mind.

[22] Beginners hear about Great Completion and think that it is all
(continued...)

important key point of meditation that, in any and every of
the three contexts of abiding, moving, and knowing, you must
look piercingly in the state of fresh rigpa that is the agent of
the knowing[23].

---

[22](...continued)
about relaxing into the "natural state" as has been badly mistrans-
lated. Because of it, they lead a relaxed and probably happy life
but do not actually get down to the very hard work required for
this kind of meditation to be effective. They end up living in a
generally happy state of samsaric confusion. In the higher levels
of practice, mindfulness is discarded because it is part of dualistic
mind. However, for the beginner, it is important even though it
is dualistic mind; mindfulness is needed to keep oneself on track
and get on with the practice and not just fall off into a relaxed but
samsaric state.

[23] You cannot afford to be lazy about the practice. Mind can be
summed up into either being still or moving and as having a
knower that knows which of the two it is doing. The knower is
called "rigpa" but here it just means a dualistic, general form of
the stripped down rigpa of the Thorough Cut practice. Thorough Cut requires that every state of mind during meditation be
taken into a fresh rigpa of the stripped down sort. That way, the
rigpa that is the agent doing the knowing—the third of the three
of abiding, moving, and knowing—ceases to be part of dualistic
mind and becomes the fresh stripped down rigpa of the Thorough Cut. A beginner will tend to space out and be in abiding or
moving dualistic type of mind and will not cut through so that the
knower of that abiding or moving becomes a non-dualistic
knower.

When you have that kind of meditation because rigpa is standing firm[24], it might seem to you that discursive thought is coming on more wildly than before and that afflicted thoughts have increased, and you might have an infinite variety of the temporary experiences of bliss, clarity, no thought, and so on start to appear. Rather than engaging in any hope and fear, suppression and furtherance[25], or clinging and grasping, look piercingly at the rigpa that is the agent of their appearance and meditate, and that will cause them to come on as assistants. If clinging and grasping occurs, you have become bound.

When the awareness becomes exceptionally sunken and dull, the clarity factor of the rigpa is not coming on. If that happens, visualize an A or a ball of light at your heart centre then send it out above your crown to a distance of about one full arrow-length and meditate on it hovering there in space. Holding the wind outside like that will dispel the problem. If the awareness becomes very wild, relax your body and

---

[24] Rigpa is able, because of the practice, to stay there and not just be lost. The rigpa is now driving the practice.

[25] Tib. dgag sgrub. "Suppression-furtherance" is the way that dualistic mind approaches the path to enlightenment. With it, you have states of mind regarded as ones to be discarded so you take the approach of attempting to suppress or stop them and you have states of mind regarded as ones to be developed, so you take the approach of trying to go further with and develop them. These two poles represent the way that dualistic mind always works with itself. Thorough Cut practice goes beyond that duality.

mind, lower your gaze, and meditate on a small sphere at the tip of the nose and that will dispel it.

Furthermore, sometimes when there is an exceptionally clear, cloudless sky, face so that the sun is behind you, aim your eyes into the centre of the sky, and hold the winds, very soothed, outside. By doing so, for an instant the dharmakaya of naked, transparently seen, empty rigpa will shine forth. This is a supremely profound foremost instruction called "the mind of the three linked spaces"[26].

Also, with the body in the Seven Dharmas and the breath's wind left natural, put your mind into absence of thought for a moment or two then lie supine on your back with your legs and arms held extended and eyes aimed into space. Express three strong "HA"s and send the wind outside. Through this, mind is can stand on its own which causes the mind of dharmatā, free from concept, to shine forth.

Also, with the body in the key points of the Seven Dharmas, and so on so that, like before, it is being left natural, rather than put yourself right on the appearance of whatever appears, put yourself right on the empty side, and with no outer, inner, or in-between, adjust your view to the shimmering,

---

[26] Tib. nam mkha' sum phrug. "The three linked spaces". This is a profound practice of the Thorough Cut that links outer, inner, and secret levels of space together into one. It has most unfortunately been translated as "sky gazing". For a person who has obtained the teaching on the practice, the correct name carries the full import of the teaching on it. The mis-translation destroys the meaning.

wiggling that you see[27]. By doing that, realization of the empty aspect, like space, will shine forth.

Also, rather than putting yourself right on the empty side, put yourself in a state of appearance that is self-illumination without grasping[28]; through that a realization of the blip, blip of appearances[29] without grasping will shine forth.

Also, having brought forth pure rigpa, turn to the emission and absorption of thought as it happens; through that a realization of thoughts being liberated in lack of support, lack of grasping[30], like waves dissolving into water, will shine forth.

These are rapidly-induced experiences[31] so they are profound methods for generating certainty in the mindstream.

---

[27] This is not a hidden way of talking about Direct Crossing practice. It is an extension of the first of these practices in which one is staring into the sky.

[28] Appearance is being allowed to occur, is known by itself, and there is no dualistic grasping in the process.

[29] The ticking over of appearance, one blip after another.

[30] "Lack of support" means that they do not come from anything in particular. "Lack of grasping" is that they can come and go without dualistic grasping being present.

[31] They are experiences of realization that are deliberately induced. Because they actually do cause the realization of the innate to manifest on the spot, they are very effective methods that quickly and easily generate a certainty about rigpa in the mindstream.

In short, the rigpa discussed so far is a mind self-abiding in its own absorption[32], alpha purity, dharmas ended; is beyond virtue and evil, faults and good qualities; is divorced from the change involved in the shifts that accompany accomplishment and making something evident; is wisdom beyond grasped-grasping rational mind; is the ultimate conveyor of the minds of the three—Madhyamaka, Mahamudra, and Mahasamdhi. It is on at all times so you simply recognize it and then, having recognized it, there is the specific activity done in order to stay in its state which is that, rather than going into a broad flatness that comes from distractedness due to loss of tightening, it is preserved it in a yoga of continuous flow of its being left natural, uncontrived[33]. That is the essence of the practice summed up.

When doing that practice, whichever consciousness of the six-fold group[34], thought of the five poisons, or temporary

---

[32] Tib. bsam gtan. Concentrated absorption.

[33] Tib. phyal ba. This term means a vast, even, empty-like space which is one of the mistaken approaches to Thorough Cut practice. It is similar to the first of the four mistaken ways to meditate that he mentioned earlier. You could call it "spacing out" which happens because of believing that Thorough Cut means to just relax and relax; by doing so, the necessary tightness of practice that maintains non-distraction from the actual rigpa is lost and that is what is being mentioned here. Instead of that, one preserves the state of actual rigpa which is to engage in a joining to—a yoga of—a continuous flow of the rigpa that comes by just leaving it to be what it is, leaving it unaltered in every way.

[34] The six consciousness that, as a group, make up human con-
(continued...)

experience that rises and falls[35] shines forth, it is, like rainbows in the sky and waves on water, the play of rigpa-bodhichitta's liveliness[36] shining forth. If comes as appearance, it equivalent to appearance; if comes as empty, it is equivalent to empty; if it comes as true, it is equivalent to true; if it is false, it is equivalent to false[37]. All of it is nothing other than the apparitions of rigpa therefore, you relax permeating it all and without grasping in the state of fresh rigpa, the agent of the shining forth, with no involvement whatsoever in suppression and furtherance, adoption and rejection, discards and antidotes, clinging and grasping, and that is how you approach the training up of the realization of whatever shines forth self-liberates[38].

---

[34](...continued)
sciousness as a whole.

[35] Bliss, clarity, no thought, and so on.

[36] Here the output of the rigpa is being emphasized. In terms of training, that output needs to correspond to enlightenment mind, that is, bodhichitta.

[37] Whichever way it comes it is just that and no more but all of it ...

[38] So far he has talked about the realizing rigpa to begin with then working on that rigpa in a simple way. Now in this paragraph he sums up the more advanced level of training which is that the offput or output of the rigpa has to be trained, too. It is done in the way that he says, which is summed up under several types of self-liberation, the first of which is self-liberation upon shining forth mentioned here.

At that time, the abiding factor is designated as "shamatha" and the realization factor of the naked, transparent rigpa'ing-emptiness is designated as "vipashyana" but their individual facts[39] are inseparable.

The entity of rigpa[40] is realized to be emptiness so one is liberated from the extreme of permanence. The nature of it[41] is seen as luminosity so one is liberated from the extreme of nihilism. Through having no hope that the temporary experiences of bliss, clarity, and no thought will come in meditation, one is liberated from the levels of the three realms[42]. Grasping involved with antidotes has collapsed so one does not stay with a disposition that is concerned with

---

[39] Tib. don. Here, "fact" means a thing known. You can explain the practice of rigpa in terms of shamatha-vipashyana as he has just done. However, if you try to find these two as individual items that you could know, you will not be able to do so because they inseparable.

[40] The entity is what rigpa is. For example a horse is a horse. Rigpa when you get down to it is empty.

[41] What the entity does. A horse runs and jumps. Rigpa does what? It knows; that is its nature. That knowing is referred to as luminosity for various reasons.

[42] Wanting bliss leads to birth in the desire realm, wanting clarity leads to birth in the formless realm. Wanting no thought leads to birth in the formless realm. If you train yourself out of wanting them by having no hope for these experiences in the practice of meditation, then you simultaneously train yourself out of the karmic habit of birth in the three realms.

deviations and obscurations[43]. Rather than maintaining hopes that come from the cage of rational-mind-made mental analysis of an enlightenment in the future, you use this approach of making the fact that the three kayas are inherently part of you into the path is the dharma which is Great Completion's special feature.

A yogin who has realized that has mental happiness, no matter how he lives, that shines forth brilliantly from within.

All obstructors[44] and points of deviation[45] arise from hope and fear, grasping and clinging to truth thus it is important to not cling to anything at all.

If the body is sick or mind is suffering and afflictions are coming with plain[46] clinging and grasping, suppression and

---

[43] Conventional meditation works on the basis that there are problem spots of mind and they should be eliminated using the appropriate antidote. Problem spots will bring points of going the wrong way—deviations—in practice and they will also mean that you could become obscured if someone or something hits that problem spot and activates it. Thorough Cut practice goes right past all of that because all of that comes only within dualistic style of mind and rigpa is non-dualistic.

[44] Tib. gegs. Obstructors are those forces that get in the way of and disrupt or stop the practice.

[45] Tib. gol sa. Points of deviation are those places at which one goes the wrong way in the practice.

[46] Tib. rang mtshan pa. Plain means just what they are in their
(continued...)

furtherance, then regardless of which way it is happening, the
fact that it is happening is identified and, then, blessings are
brought down by supplicating the guru. Having done that
one thing, the awareness involved with suppression and furtherance is examined not superficially but very precisely to
find where it comes from, where it dwells, and where it goes
to, and so on. If that is done, you find that the awareness does
not exist anywhere at all and does not abide as anything in
particular. It is not possible that wisdom, the naked empty
rigpa's dharmakaya, that goes un-demonstrated with the
words "here, it is this" because of being beyond the grasped-
grasping process of rational mind, would not shine forth.
Thus, its shining forth and the preservation of its state will
cause obstructors and points of deviation in their entirety to
go into self-liberation.

The king of all enhancers[47] is devotion to the guru so aban-
don the mind that apprehends the guru as an ordinary person
and cherish not being separated from the faith and devotion
which see him as an actual buddha. Furthermore, if you
meditate to carry out development of the minds of imperma-
nence, compassion, development stage, and completion stage
with and without signs, there is great value that can be brought out bit by bit that can take you exceptionally far through
the levels[48].

---

[46](...continued)
samsaric glory; ordinary, gunky, samsara.

[47] See glossary.

[48] This does relate to the first sentence because value mentioned
(continued...)

Then, at the end of sessions, do not part from doing dedications and, in between sessions, do not part from carrying all dharmas onto the path through seeing them as illusory.

Then at night-time, there is the yoga of sleep. Lying down, supplicate for sleep to be luminosity, then mix the guru's mind with yours and preserve the state of fresh rigpa; not letting other discursive thought create a barrier, fall asleep.

Furthermore, the key points for you to be aware of are as follows. If the view does not take you across, it means that grasped-grasping which is the fetter of clinging to truth has not collapsed, so in the context of equipoise, you cherish being taken across only into the flatness of absence of all dharmas in spontaneous existence[49]. If you do not preserve the state of meditation, you are not going along right over the key point of being just what is, so it is important to persevere at lengthening the duration of the state. If you do not part

---

[48](...continued)

in this section is another word for what enhancers bring out. In other words, you could also see all conventional style practice as enhancement practice and that could be very good to do if you want to do it, because these conventional meditations which in themselves are enhancers of a sort, can take you very far. Conventional, enhancer practice is not bad to do, though it is not part of Thorough Cut.

[49] He is talking about the view. If your view as you have it is not taking you across, then you have a dualistic view, still. The view that you should cherish as the one that takes you across is the one in which there is the vast flatness of emptiness unified with spontaneous presence of appearance.

sides with conduct, then is the great danger of falling in bad behaviour because of claiming that virtue is empty and evil-doing is empty, so there is the key point that, in post-attainment, having allied yourself with illusoriness, your firm confidence in the infallibility of cause and effect transforms anything that you do into virtuous action. If method and prajna become two separate items, you are bound at all times, so it is important to engage in the good path given out by the conquerors, in which one joins the two of emptiness and compassion and the two accumulation of merit and wisdom into unification.

These are very important headings that should be highly cherished so please, I ask you, to plant them in your mind as such.

> If impermanence and disenchantment have not
>   been produced in my mindstream,
> Practice done with a mere semblance of it
> Will not be a time of true accomplishment of the
>   holy dharma;
> May I produce an uncontrived renunciation in
>   mind.

> If I do not train well in compassion and bodhichitta,
> I'll be in the dark tracts of a mind that thinks only
>   of its own sake
> And then there will be no chance for the excellent
>   path of the Great Vehicle to appear,
> Therefore, may I connect with authentic
>   bodhichitta.

Not having attained to a noble one[50], I'll have a
    semblance only of thought for others' sakes—
It does not benefit others and is a cause for being
    bound myself so
Instead of spinning my head with entertainments
    and distractions,
May I persevere at practice in an isolated place.

Method and prajna as two separate items is like a
    person with legs broken—
The power for journeying through the levels and
    paths of full knowledge[51] has ended so
May I engage in the un-mistaken path of joining
    together
Emptiness and compassion, development and
    completion stages, and the two accumulations.

If there is no transmission of blessings from a guru
    with lineage,

---

[50] Tib. 'phags pa. Noble ones are those who, having exited samsara, are no longer touched by it themselves. Thus they are
capable of assisting others to exit in a way that would never be
mistaken or misguided. Beings still in samsara can help others to
exit but there is the likelihood that they will, due to still having an
idea of themselves, lead the other person in a mistaken way and
bind themselves further at the same time.

[51] The levels and paths that belong to the path of the full knowledge that is buddhahood.

The resulting meditation that imposes suffering[52]
    will not bring realization of actuality so
Through the interdependency of devotion that has
    reached full measure,
May I obtain the supreme empowerment that
    transmits the mind lineage.

Self-knowing luminosity beyond rational mind, the
    Greater Completion,
Kayas and wisdom, primordial spontaneous
    existence,
Bring the foremost instruction[53] of the four Chog
    Zhag[54] of how things are;

---

[52] If you do not have this kind of guru who can give the special transmission of non-dual practice, any meditation you do will be conventional meditation and will, because it is still within concept, be pinching you and making you suffer, even though it is meant to be the way out. Unconventional practices like Thorough Cut do not have that fault. The way to succeed in Thorough Cut is, as he mentioned at the beginning, to supplicate a guru who does have the necessary lineage. The interdependency of that guru with his blessings and your making supplications to him can lead to the transmission of the mind lineage and that is the supreme empowerment which opens your mind directly and on the spot to the ultimate meaning.

[53] See the glossary.

[54] See the glossary.

May they result in seizing the stronghold at the
level of exhaustion[55].

Some time, when the level at which I can benefit
migrators has been obtained,
With the needed armour for others' sake of not
wearying and being patient,
May I alone take the mothers equal to space
Across the river of becoming to complete
liberation.

*The carefree yogin with happy mind instructed his friend named
Kamali. The instructions are a medicinal foremost instruction for
beginners. The end. ITHI.*

---

[55] He does not say "Great Completion". There is a reason for it.
This is pointing out one aspect of Great Completion and it is the
aspect that gives the name Great Completion. So it is not the
whole story but the greater part of it. The other part is the spontaneous presence mentioned in the next line. The two together
mean that there are buddhas who teach the teachings. The
teaching of Thorough Cut is summed up in their teaching with
the Four Chog Zhags, meaning the four ways of being just so:
view, meditation, conduct, and rigpa or fruition. If you have
those instructions come from primordial reality like that, then
you could pray to gain the stronghold, the place that could not be
defeated and which has power over everything underneath, of the
final realization of Thorough Cut in which all dualistic dharmas
have been totally exhausted. This verse has a lot of meaning in its
arrangement. It goes from the most primordial state down into
samsara and comes back again.

GLOSSARY

Actuality, Tib. gnas lugs: A key term in both sutra and tantra and one of a pair of terms, the other being apparent reality (Tib. snang lugs). The two terms are used when determining the reality of a situation. The actuality of any given situation is how (lugs) the situation actuality sits or is present (gnas); the apparent reality is how any given situation appears to an observer. Something could appear in many different ways, depending on the circumstances at the time and on the being perceiving it but, regardless of those circumstances, it will always have its own actuality, how it really is. The term actuality is frequently used in Mahāmudrā and Great Completion teachings to mean the fundamental reality of any given phenomenon or situation before any deluded mind alters it and makes it appear differently.

Affliction, Skt. kleśha, Tib. nyon mongs: This term is usually translated as emotion or disturbing emotion, etcetera but Buddha was very specific about the meaning of this word. When the Buddha referred to the emotions, meaning a movement of mind, he did not refer to them as such but called them "kleśha" in Sanskrit, meaning exactly "affliction". It is a basic part of the Buddhist teaching that emotions afflict

23

beings, giving them problems at the time and causing more problems in the future.

Alaya, Tib. kun gzhi: This term, if translated, is usually translated as all-base or thereabouts. It is a Sanskrit term that means a range that underlies and forms a basis for something else. In Buddhist teaching, it means a particular level of mind that sits beneath all other levels of mind. However, it is used in several different ways in the Buddhist teaching and changes to a different meaning in case. In the Great Completion teachings, a distinction is made between alaya and alaya consciousness; the distinction is subtle but the two must not be confused.

Alpha purity, Tib. ka dag: A Great Completion term meaning purity that is there from the first, that is, primordial purity. There are many terms in Buddhism that express the notion of "primordial purity" but this one is unique to the Great Completion teaching. Some people do not like the term "alpha purity" but this is exactly what the Tibetan says.

Alteration, altered, same as contrivance q.v.

Assurance, Tib. gdeng: Although often translated as confidence, this term means assurance with all of the extra meaning conveyed by that term. A bird might be confident of its ability to fly but more than that, it has the assurance that it will not fall to the ground because of knowing that it has wings and the training to use them. Similarly, a person might be confident that they could liberate the afflictions but not assured of doing so because of lack of training or other causes. However, a person who has accumulated the causes to be able to liberate afflictions trained is assured of the ability to do so.

Bliss, clarity, and no-thought, Tib. bde gsal mi rtog pa: A practitioner who engages in practice will have signs of that practice appear as various types of temporary experience. Most commonly, three types of experience are met with: bliss, clarity, and no-thought. Bliss is ease of the body and-or mind, clarity is heightened knowing of mind, and no-thought is an absence of thought that happens in the mind. The three are usually mentioned when discussing the passing experiences that arise because of practising meditation but there is also a way of describing them as final experiences of realization.

Chog Zhag, Tib. cog bzhag: The teaching on four Chog Zhag is part of the Thorough Cut teaching of Great Completion. The four Chog Zhag are four ways of being in which the practitioner has put himself chog zhag, meaning "set just so". The four are mountain, ocean, appearances, and rigpa. They show they way of being that is taught in the Thorough Cut practice; they can be used as an introduction to that practice but also to give profound instruction on the details of the practice.

Clarity or Illumination, Skt. vara, Tib. gsal ba: When you see this term, it should be understood as an abbreviation of the full term in Tibetan, 'od gsal ba, which is usually translated as luminosity. It is not another factor of mind distinct from luminosity but merely a convenient abbreviation in both Indian and Tibetan dharma language for the longer term, luminosity. See "Luminosity" in this glossary for more.

Clinging, Tib. zhen pa: In Buddhism, this term refers specifically to the twofold process of dualistic mind mis-taking things that are not true, not pure, as true, pure, etcetera and then, because of seeing them as highly desirable even though they are not, attaching itself to or clinging to those things. This type of clinging acts as a kind of glue that keeps you with the unsatisfactory things of cyclic existence because of mistakenly seeing them as desirable.

Confusion, Tib. 'khrul pa: In Buddhism, this term mostly refers to the fundamental confusion of taking things the wrong way that happens because of fundamental ignorance though it can also have the more general meaning of having lots of thoughts and being confused about it. In the first case, it is defined like this, "Confusion is the appearance to rational mind of something being present when it is not", and refers for example to seeing an object, such as a table, as being truly present when in fact it is present only as mere, interdependent appearance.

Contrivance, contrived, Tib. bcos pa: A term meaning that something has been altered from its native state.

Cyclic existence, Skt. saṃsāra, Tib. 'khor ba: The type of existence that sentient beings have which is that they continue on from one existence to another, always within the enclosure of births that are produced by ignorance and experienced as unsatisfactory. Although the Tibetan term literally means "cycling", the original Sanskrit has a slightly different meaning; it means to go about, here and there.

Dharmakaya, Tib. chos sku: The mind of a buddha. Dharma here means reality, what actually is, and kāya means body.

Dharmata, Tib. chos nyid: A Sanskrit term used to refer to the reality of any given situation. Thus, there are many dharmatās. The term is often used in Buddhism to refer to general reality that underlies all types of existence but that is not its only meaning. For example, even the fact of water's wetness can be referred to as the dharmatā of water, meaning water's reality in general. The term is similar to "actuality" (Tib. gnas lugs).

Dhyana, Tib. bsam gtan: A Sanskrit term meaning all types of mental absorption. Mental absorptions cultivated in the human realm generally result in births in the form realms which are deep forms of concentration in themselves. The practices of mental absorption done in the human realm and the godly existences of the form realm that result from them both are named "dhyāna". The Buddha repeatedly pointed out that the dhyānas were a side-track to emancipation from cyclic existence.

Discursive thought, Skt. vikalpita, Tib. rnam rtog: This means more than just the superficial thought that is heard as a voice in the head. It includes the entirety of conceptual process that arises due to mind contacting any object of any of the senses. The Sanskrit and Tibetan literally mean "(dualistic) thought (that arises from the mind wandering among the) various (superficies perceived in the doors of the senses)".

Elaboration, Tib. spro ba: to be producing thoughts.

Enhancer, Tib. bogs 'don. A means by which some realization that has not been turned out yet in the practitioner's experience is now brought forth. The as yet unexposed possibilities in the experience that a practitioner has developed are brought forth into plain view by these techniques.

Thorough Cut is special in that it is usually said not to have enhancers. The reason for this is that if you have realized— meaning directly recognized—rigpa, then that is it and there is no more to be seen. It is a key point concerning rigpa practice. However, if you were to talk about an enhancer for the practice as a whole, it would have to be devotion to the guru because that is one the means by which the transmission of blessings necessary for the realization of rigpa occurs.

Enlightenment mind, Skt. bodhicitta, Tib. byang chub sems: A key term of the Great Vehicle. It is the type of mind that is connected not with the lesser enlightenment of an arhat but the enlightenment of a truly complete buddha. As such, it is a mind that is connected with the aim of bringing all sentient beings to that same level of buddhahood. A person who has this mind has entered the Great Vehicle and is either a bodhisatva or a buddha.

It is important to understand that the term is used to refer equally to the minds of all levels of bodhisatva on the path to buddhahood and to the mind of a buddha who has completed the path. Therefore it is not "mind striving for enlightenment" as is so often translated but "enlightenment mind", that kind of mind which is connected with the full enlightenment of a truly complete buddha and which is present in all those who belong to the Great Vehicle. The term is used in the conventional Great Vehicle and also in the Vajra Vehicle. In the Vajra Vehicle, there are some special uses of the term where substances of the pure aspect of the subtle physical body are understood to be manifestations of enlightenment mind.

Entity, Tib. ngo bo: The entity of something is just exactly what that thing is. In English we would often simply say "thing" rather than entity but there is the problem that, in Buddhism, "thing" has a very specific meaning and not the general meaning that it has in English. See also under Essence in this glossary.

Equipoise and post-attainment, Tib. mnyam bzhag and rjes thob: Although often called "meditation and post-meditation", the actual term is "equipoise and post-attainment". There is great meaning in the actual wording which is lost by the looser translation.

Essence, Tib. ngo bo: This is a key term used throughout Buddhist theory. The original in Sanskrit and the term in Tibetan, too, has both meanings of "essence" and "entity". In some situations the term has more the first meaning and in others, the second. For example, when speaking of mind and mind's essence, it is referring to the core or essential part within mind. On the other hand, when speaking of something such as fire, one can speak of the entity, fire, and its characteristics, such as heat, and so on; in this case, the term does not mean essence but means that thing, what is actually is.

Exaggeration, Tib. skur 'debs pa: In Buddhism, this term is used in two ways. Firstly, it is used in general to mean misunderstanding from the perspective that one has added more to one's understanding of something than needs to be there. Secondly, it is used specifically to indicate that dualistic mind always overstates or exaggerates whatever object it is examining. Dualistic mind always adds the ideas of solidity, permanence, singularity, and so on to everything it references via the concepts that it uses. Severing of exaggeration either means removal of these un-necessary understandings when trying to properly comprehend something or removal of the dualistic process altogether when trying to get to the non-dualistic reality of a phenomenon.

Fictional, Skt. saṃvṛti, Tib. kun rdzob: This term is paired with the term "superfactual" q.v. Until now these two terms have been translated as "relative" and "absolute" but the translations are nothing like the original terms. These terms are extremely important in the Buddhist teaching so it is very important that they be corrected but more than that, if the actual meaning of these terms is not presented, then the teaching connected with them cannot be understood.

The Sanskrit term saṃvṛti means a deliberate invention, a fiction, a hoax. It refers to the mind of ignorance which, because of being obscured and so not seeing suchness, is not true but a fiction. The things that appear to the ignorance are therefore fictional. Nonetheless, the beings who live in this ignorance believe that the things that appear to them through the filter of ignorance are true, are real. Therefore, these beings live in fictional truth.

Fictional truth, Skt. saṃvṛtisatya, Tib. kun rdzob bden pa: See under "Fictional" for an explanation of this term.

Foremost instruction, Skt. upadeśa, Tib. man ngag: there are several types of instruction mentioned in Buddhist literature: there is the general level of instruction which is the meaning contained in the words of the texts of the tradition; on a more personal and direct level there is oral instruction which has been passed down from teacher to student from the time of the buddha; and on the most profound level there is upadeśa which are not only oral instructions provided by one's guru but are special, core instructions that come out of personal experience and which convey the teaching concisely and with the full weight of personal experience. Upadeśa are crucial to the Vajra Vehicle because these are the special way of passing on the profound instructions needed for the student's realization.

Grasped-grasping, Tib. gzung 'dzin: When mind is turned outwardly as it is in the normal operation of dualistic mind, it has developed two faces that appear simultaneously. Special names are given to these two faces: mind appearing in the form of the external object being referenced is called "that which is grasped". Mind appearing in the form of the consciousness that is referencing it is called "the grasper" or "grasping" of it. Thus, there is the pair of terms "grasped-grasper" or "grasped-grasping". When these two terms are used, it alerts you immediately to the fact that a Mind Only style of presentation is being discussed. This pair of terms pervades Mind Only, Madhyamaka, and tantric writings and is exceptionally important in all of them.

Note that you could substitute the word "apprehended" for "grasped" and "apprehender" for "grasper" or "grasping" and that would reflect one connotation of the original Indian terminology. The solidified duality of grasped and grasper is nothing but an invention of dualistic thought. It has that kind of character or characteristic.

Great Vehicle, Skt. mahāyāna, Tib. theg pa chen po: The Buddha's teachings as a whole can be summed up into three vehicles where a vehicle is defined as that which can carry you to a certain destination. The first vehicle, called the Lesser Vehicle, contains the teachings designed to get an individual moving on the spiritual path through showing the unsatisfactory state of cyclic existence and an emancipation from that. However, that path is only concerned with personal emancipation and fails to take account of all of the beings that there are in existence. There used to be eighteen schools of Lesser Vehicle in India but the only one surviving these days is the Theravada of south-east Asia. The Greater Vehicle is a step up from that. The Buddha explained that it was great in comparison to the Lesser Vehicle for seven reasons. The first of those is that it is concerned with attaining the truly complete enlightenment of a truly complete buddha for the sake of every sentient being where the Lesser Vehicle is concerned only with a personal liberation that is not truly complete enlightenment and which is achieved only for the sake of that practitioner. The Great Vehicle has two divisions. There is a conventional Great Vehicle in which the path is taught in a logical, conventional way. There is also an unconventional Great Vehicle in which the path is taught in an unconventional and very direct way. This latter vehicle is called the Vajra Vehicle because it takes the innermost, indestructible (vajra) fact of reality of one's own mind as the vehicle to enlightenment.

Key points, Tib. gnad: Key points are those places in one's being that one works, like pressing buttons, in order to get some desired effect. For example, in meditation, there are key points of the body; by adjusting those key points, the mind is brought closer to reality and the meditation is thus assisted.

In general, this term is used in Buddhist meditation instruction but it is, in particular, part of the special vocabulary of the Great Completion teachings. Overall, the Great Completion teachings are given as a series of key points that must be attended to in order to bring forth the various realizations of the path.

Liveliness, Tib. rtsal: A key term in both Mahāmudrā and Great Completion. The term means the ability that something has to express itself. In the case of rigpa, it refers to how the rigpa actually comes out into expression. The term is sometimes translated as "display" but that is not right. It is not merely the display that is being talked about here but the fact that something has the ability to express itself in a certain way. Another English word that fits the meaning, though one which is drier than "liveliness" is "expressivity". In the end, given the way that this term is actually used in the higher tantras, it refers to the liveliness of whatever is being referred to, usually rigpa.

Luminosity, Skt. prabhāsvara, Tib. 'od gsal ba: the core of mind, called mind's essence, has two aspects, parts, or factors as they are called. One is emptiness and the other is knowing. Luminosity is a metaphor for the fundamental knowing quality of the essence of mind. It is sometimes translated as "clear light" but that is a mistake that comes from not understanding how the words of the Sanskrit and the Tibetan, too, go together. It does not refer to a light that has the quality of clearness (something that makes no sense, actually!) but refers to the illuminative property which is the hallmark of mind. Mind knows, that is what it does. Metaphorically, it is a luminosity that illuminates its own content. In both Sanskrit and Tibetan Buddhist literature, the term is frequently abbreviated just to gsal ba, "clarity", with the same meaning.

Mind, Skt. chitta, Tib. sems: the complicated process of mind which occurs because there is ignorance. This sort of mind is a samsaric phenomenon. It is a dualistic mind.

Mindfulness, Tib. dran pa: A particular mental event, one that has the ability to keep mind on its object. Together with alertness, it is one of the two causes of developing shamatha. See alertness for a explanation.

Not stopped, Tib. ma 'gags pa: An important path term in the teaching of both Mahāmudrā and Great Completion. The essence of mind has two parts: emptiness and luminosity. Both of these must come unified. However, when a practitioner does the practice, he will fall into one extreme or the other and that is called "stoppage". The aim of the practice is to get to the stage in which there is both emptiness and luminosity together. In that case, there is no stoppage of falling into one extreme or the other. Thus non-stopped luminosity is a term that indicates that there is the luminosity with all of its appearance yet that luminosity, for the practitioner, is not mistaken, is not stopped off. Stopped luminosity is an experience like luminosity but in which the appearances have, at least to some extent, not been mixed with emptiness.

Poisons, Tib. dug: In Buddhism, poison is a general term for the afflictions. For samsaric beings, the afflictions are poisonous things which harm them. The Buddha most commonly spoke of the three poisons, which are the principal afflictions of desire, aggression, and ignorance. He also spoke of "the five poisons" which is a slightly longer enumeration of the principal afflictions: desire, aggression, delusion, pride, and jealousy.

Post-attainment, Tib. rjes thob: See "Equipoise and post-attainment".

Prajna, Tib. shes rab: A Sanskrit term for the type of mind that makes good and precise distinctions between this and that and hence which arrives at good understanding. It is sometimes translated as "wisdom" but that is not correct because it is, generally speaking, a mental event belonging to dualistic mind where "wisdom" is generally used to refer to the non-dualistic knower of a Buddha. Moreover, the main feature of prajna is its ability to distinguish correctly between one thing and another and hence to have a good understanding. It is very much part of intellect.

Preserve, Tib. skyong ba: An important term in both Mahāmudrā and Great Completion. In general, it means to defend, protect, nurture, maintain. In the higher tantras it means to keep something just as it is, to nurture that something so that it stays and is not lost. Also, in the higher tantras, it is often used in reference to preserving the state where the state is some particular state of being. Because of this, the phrase "preserve the state" is an important instruction in the higher tantras.

Proliferation, Tib. 'phro ba: A term meaning that the dualistic mind has become active and is giving off thoughts. This is actually the same word as "elaboration" but is the intransitive sense.

Rational mind, Tib. blo: The Kagyu and Nyingma traditions use this term pejoratively for the most part. In the Great Completion and Mahāmudrā teachings, this term specifically means the dualistic mind. It is the villain, so to speak, which needs to be removed from the equation in order to obtain enlightenment. This term is commonly translated simply as mind but that causes confusion with the many other words that are also translated simply as mind. It is not just another mind but is specifically the sort of mind that creates the situation of this and that (ratio in Latin) and hence upholds the duality of samsara. It is the very opposite of the essence of mind. Thus, this is a key term which should be noted and not just glossed over as "mind".

Rigpa, Tib. rig pa: This is the singularly most important term in the whole of Great Completion and Mahāmudrā. In particular, it is the key word of all words in the Great Completion system of the Thorough Cut. Rigpa literally means to know in the sense of "I see!" It is used at all levels of meaning from the coarsest everyday sense of knowing something to the deepest sense of knowing something as presented in the system of Thorough Cut. The system of Thorough Cut uses this term in a very special sense, though it still retains its basic meaning of "to know". To translate it as "awareness" which is common practice these days is a poor practice; there are many kinds of awareness but there is only one rigpa and besides, rigpa is substantially more than just awareness. Since this is such an important term and since it lacks an equivalent in English, I choose not to translate it. However, it will be helpful in reading the text to understanding the meaning as just given.

This is the term used to indicate enlightened mind as experienced by the practitioner on the path of these practices. The term itself specifically refers to the dynamic knowing quality of mind. It absolutely does not mean a simple registering, as implied by the word "awareness" which unfortunately is often used to translate this term. There is no word in English that exactly matches it, though the idea of "seeing" or "insight on the spot" is very close. Proof of this is found in the fact that the original Sanskrit term "vidyā" is actually the root of all words in English that start with "vid" and mean "to see", for example, "video", "vision", and so on. Chogyam Trungpa Rinpoche, who was particular skilled at getting Tibetan words into English, also stated that this term rigpa really did not have a good equivalent in English, though he thought that "insight" was the closest. My own conclusion after hearing extensive teaching on it is that rigpa is just best left untranslated. However, it will be helpful in reading the text to understanding the meaning as just given. Note that rigpa has both noun and verb forms. To get the verb form, I use "rigpa'ing".

Secret Mantra, Tib. gsang sngags: Another name for the Vajra Vehicle or the tantric teachings.

Seven Dharmas of Vairochana, Tib. rnam par snang mdzad chos bdun: These are the seven aspects of Vairochana's posture, the posture used for formal meditation practice. The posture for the legs is the one called "vajra posture" or vajrāsana. In it, the legs are crossed one on top of the other, right on top of left. The advantage of this posture is that, of the five basic winds of the subtle body, the downward-clearing wind is caused to enter the central channel. The posture for the hands is called the equipoise mudrā. The right palm is placed on top of the left palm and the two thumbs are just touching, raised up over the palms. The advantage of this posture is that the Fire-Accompanying Wind is caused to enter the central channel. The posture for the spine is that the spine should be held straight. The advantage of this posture is that the Pervader Wind is caused to enter the central channel. The posture for the shoulders is one in which the shoulders are held up slightly in a particular way. The advantage of this posture is that Upward-Moving Wind is caused to enter the central channel. The neck and chin are held in a particular posture: the neck is drawn up a little and the chin slightly hooked in towards the throat. The advantage of this posture is that the Life-Holder Wind is caused to enter the central channel. The tip of the tongue is joined with the forward part of the palate and the jaws are relaxed, with the teeth and lips allowed to sit normally. The eyes are directed down past the tip of the nose, into space. Placing the gaze in this way keeps the clarity of mind and prevents sinking, agitation, and so on.

State, Tib. ngang: A key term in Mahāmudrā and Great Completion. Unfortunately it is often not translated and in so doing much meaning is lost. Alternatively, it is often translated as "within" which is incorrect. The term means a "state". A state is a certain, ongoing situation. In Buddhist meditation in general, there are various states that a practitioner has to enter and remain in as part of developing the meditation.

Temporary experience, Tib. nyams: The practice of meditation brings with it various experiences that happen simply because of the meditation. These experiences are temporary experiences and not the final, unchanging experience, of realization.

Thorough Cut, Tib. khregs chod: the Dzogchen system has several levels to it. The innermost level has two main practices, the first called Thregcho which literally translates as Thorough Cut and the second called Thogal which translates as Direct Crossing. The meaning of Thorough Cut has been misunderstood. The meaning is clearly explained in the *Illuminator Tibetan-English Dictionary*:

> "Thorough Cut is a practice in which the solidification that sentient beings produce by having rational minds which grasp at a perceived object and perceiving subject is sliced through so as to get the underlying reality which has always been present in the essence of mind and which is called Alpha Purity in this system of teachings. For this reason, Thorough Cut is also known as Alpha Purity Thorough Cut."

The etymology of the word is explained in the Great Completion teachings either as ཁྲེགས་སུ་ཆོད་པ་ or ཁྲེགས་གི་ཆོད་པ་. In either case, the term ཆོད་པ་ is "a cut"; there are all sorts of different "cuts" and this is one of them. Then, in the case of ཁྲེགས་སུ་ཆོད་པ་, ཁྲེགས་སུ་ is an adverb modifying the verb "to cut" and has the meaning of making the cut fully, completely. It is explained with the example of slicing off a finger. A finger could be sliced with a sharp knife such that the cut was not quite complete and the cut off portion was left hanging. Alternatively, it could be sliced through in one, decisive movement such that the finger was completely and definitely severed. That kind of thorough cut is what is meant here. In the case of ཁྲེགས་གི་ཆོད་པ་, the term ཁྲེགས་གི་ is as an adverb that has the meaning of something that is doubtless, of something that is unquestionably so. A translation based on the first explanation would be "Thorough Cut" and on the second would be "Decisive Cut".

Other translations that have been put forward for this term are: "Cutting Resistance" and "Cutting Solidity". Of these, "Cutting Resistance" is usually a translation made on the basis of students expressing the "resistance to practice", etcetera. That is a complete misunderstanding of the term. The term means that that the practitioner of this system cuts *decisively* through rational mind, regardless of its degree of solidity, so as to arrive directly at the essence of mind.

Transparency, Tib. zang thal: This term belongs to the unique vocabulary of Great Completion. It has two connotations: that something is seen directly, in direct perception; and that it is seen with full visibility because there is no agent obscuring the view of it. The term is used to indicate that rigpa is truly present for the practitioner. Luminosity when it is the rigpa of the enlightened side and not the not-rigpa, usually translated as ignorance, of the samsaric side, has transparency or, you could say, full visibility, as one of its qualities precisely because it has none of the factors of mind as such in it, which would obscure it. Transparency means that the rigpa is in full view: it really is rigpa seen in direct perception and it is without rational mind so it is seen without any of the obscuring factors that would make it less than immediately and fully visible.

Unaltered or uncontrived, Tib. ma bcos pa: The opposite of "altered" and "contrived". Something which has not been altered from its native state; something which has been left just as it is.

Upadesha, Tib. man ngag: See the glossary entry "Foremost Instruction".

View, meditation, and conduct, Tib. lta sgom spyod: A formulation of the teachings that contains all of the meaning of the path.

Vipashyana, Tib. lhag mthong: The Sanskrit name for one of the two main practices of meditation needed in the Buddhist system for gaining insight into reality. The other one, shamatha, keeps the mind focussed while this one, vipashyanā, looks piercingly into the nature of things.

Wisdom, Skt. jñāna, Tib. ye shes: This is a fruition term that refers to the kind of mind, the kind of knower possessed by a buddha. The original Sanskrit term has many meanings but overall has the sense of just knowing. In Buddhism, it refers to the most basic type of knowing possible. Sentient beings could do this but their minds are obscured so, although they have the potential for knowing with the wisdom of a buddha, it does not happen. If they practise the path to buddhahood, at some point they will leave behind their obscuration and start knowing in this very simple and immediate way.

This sort of knowing is there at the core of every being's mind. Therefore, the Tibetans called it "the particular type of awareness which is always there". Because of their wording, it is often called "primordial wisdom" but that is too much. It simply means wisdom in the sense of the most fundamental knowing possible.

TIBETAN TEXT

༄༅། །ཞེ་ཆེན་རྒྱལ་ཚབ་རིན་པོ་ཆེས་མཛད་པའི་ཉམས་ལེན་གྱི་
མདོ་འགགག་བཞུགས་སོ།།

༄༅། །རྒྱལ་བ་གཉིས་པ་དཔལ་བསམ་ཡས་པ་ཀུན་མཁྱེན་ངག་གི་དབང་
པོ་ལ་ཕྱག་འཆལ་ལོ། །དེ་ལ་སྐབས་སུ་བབས་པའི་ཉམས་ལེན་གྱི་མདོ་འགགག་
ཅུང་ཟད་བཤད་ན། ཐོག་མར་བདེ་བའི་སྟུན་ལ་ལུས་གནད་རྣམ་སྣང་ཆོས་
བདུན་བདེ་ལྷུགས་སུ་སྟྦྱིད་ཆ་དང་བཅས་པར་བཅའ། ཁྱད་པར་མིག་ཡེ་ཤེས་
འཆར་བའི་སྦྲོ་ཡིན་པས་ཐད་དྲང་གི་ནམ་མཁར་རྟེན་མེད་དུ་ཏུ་རེ་བལྟ། དགག་
གནད་རླུང་རང་བབས་སུ་འབྱུང་འཇུག་ཡང་སྣ་ནས་མི་བྱ་བར་ཁ་ནས་རབ་ཏུ་
དལ་བུས་བྱ་སྟེ། འདི་དག་རེ་རེ་བཞིན་དགོས་པ་ཆེན་པོ་ཡོད་པ་ཡིན་པས་
གཡས་ཆུང་དུ་མི་གཏོང་བ་གལ་ཆེའོ། དེ་ནས་ངེས་འབྱུང་སྐྱོ་ཤས་སྐྱེད་རྗེ་
བྱང་ཆུབ་ཀྱི་སེམས་སྦྱོམ་པ་སྦྱོན་དུ་འགྲོ་བས། རང་གི་སྙི་བོར་པད་ཟླའི་སྟེང་
དུ་རྩ་བའི་བླ་མ་ཉིད་རྒྱན་ཆ་ལུགས་དགུས་མཛེ་བའི་རྣམ་པར་བསྒོམ་ལ། མོས་
གུས་མཚེ་མ་འཁྱགས་པའི་སྒོ་ནས་ཐབ་ལམ་གྱི་རྟོགས་པ་ཁྱོད་པར་ཅན་སྐྱེར་དུ་
རང་གི་རྒྱུད་ལ་སྐྱེད་པར་གསོལ་བ་གདབ། དེ་ཡང་ཁ་ཆཾ་ཆིག་ཆཾ་གྱི་མི་
ཐན་ཏེ། རྟོགས་པ་ཆེན་པོའི་རྟོགས་པ་རྒྱུད་ལ་སྐྱེ་བ་ལ་བརྒྱུད་ལྷན་བླ་མའི

41

ཐུགས་རྒྱུད་ཀྱི་ཕྲིན་ལྲབས་འཕོ་དགོས་དེ་འཕོ་བ་སྒྲུབ་པའི་མོས་གུས་ལ་རག
ལས་པའི་ཕྱིར་འདི་ཁོ་ན་གཙོ་ཆེ་བ་བཏོན་བཏོན་སྒྲུབ་སྒྲུབ་མང་པོའི་བྱས་ཡུས་མི
འཛིན་པར་ཕྱུར་ཆུགས་སུ་གསོལ་བ་འདེབས་པ་གལ་ཆེ། མཐར་དབང་བཞི
ལེན་པའི་དམིགས་གནད་དང་བཅས་བླ་མ་དང་རང་སེམས་དབྱེར་མེད་དུ་བསྲེས
ཏེ་གཤིས་བདེ་བ་ཆེན་པོ་གསལ་སྟོང་འཛིན་བྲལ་དུ་སྐྱོང་བ་སྟེ། དེའང་ཅི་ཡང
དྲན་མེད་ནག་ཐོམ་ལུང་མ་བསྟན་པ་ཀུན་གཞིའི་ངང་དེ་བསྐྱོམ་དུ་འདོད་པ་མ
ཡིན། ཀུན་གཞིའི་རྣམ་ཤེས་གསལ་རིག་ཙམ་གནས་ཆ་ཚན་དེའི་ངང་དུ
བསྐྱོམ་པ་མ་ཡིན། དེ་བཞིན་དུ་མི་རྟོག་པའི་ཉམས་ཏུད་དེ་བ་དེའི་ངང་དེ
བསྐྱོམ་དུ་འདོད་པ་མ་ཡིན། ཡུལ་དུ་ཤར་ཟིན་པའི་རྣམ་རྟོག་མི་འགྱུ་དག་འགྱུ
དེ་ཀ་བསྐྱོམ་དུ་འདོད་པ་མ་ཡིན། ཚོ་ན་གང་ཞེ་ན། རྣམ་རྟོག་སྩ་མ
འགགས། ཕྱི་མ་མ་སྐྱེས། ད་ལྟ་བ་བློའི་ཆེས་གདབ་དང་བྲལ་བའི་རང
རིག་ཟང་ཀ་མ་གསལ་སྟོང་རྗུང་འཆུག་ནམ་མཁའ་ལྟ་བུའི་དགོངས་པ་འཆར་བ
དེ། བློ་འདས་རྟོགས་པ་ཆེན་པོ་ཀ་དག་ཁྲེགས་ཆོད་ཆོས་ཟད་ཟད་ཐལ་རྗེན་པ
ཡིན་པས་དེ་ཉིད་རྟོ་ཤེས་པར་བྱས་ལ་རང་བབས་བདེ་ལྷུགས་སུ་འཇོག་པ་ལ
ཉམས་ལེན་སྐྱོང་བ་ཞེས་བྱའོ། །ལྷ་སྒོམ་སྒྱུད་གསུམ་གང་གི་སྐབས་སུའང
འདི་ཉིད་རྗེན་ལ་འབྱུད་ཤེས་དགོས། དེ་མ་ཤེས་ན་གཅིག་གིས་སྐྱེ་འགགས
གནས་གསུམ་དང་བྲལ་བར་བསྒུན། གཅིག་གིས་དེ་ལྟ་བུའི་སྐྱམ་དུ་བསམ
པས་མིང་མེད་མིང་དུ་སོང་བ་བཞིན་བློས་བྱས་ཡིད་དཔྱོད་ཀྱི་གཟེབ་ནས་ནམ
ཡང་རྟོགས་པའི་དུས་མི་ཡོང་། བློ་འདས་རིག་སྟོང་རྗེན་པའི་ཆོས་སྐུ་འདི
བཟོད་པའི་ཆེག་དང་བཏགས་དཔྱད་ཀྱི་བློས་དོན་སྤྱི་ཚམ་ལས་གཏན་ལ་འབེབས
མི་ནུས་ཀྱང་བླ་མའི་བྱིན་རླབས་དང་རང་གི་སྨོན་སྨོནས་འཚོམས་པས་རྗེ་ཞིག་ན
བྱིས་པས་བསམ་མནོ་རྟེད་པ་བཞིན་སྟོ་འདོགས་ནང་ནས་ཆོད་ཡོད་པས་མི་བསྒྱུར
བར་རྒྱུན་དུ་བཙོན་འགྲུས་ཀྱི་སྐྱོམ་པ་གལ་ཆེའོ། ལས་དང་པོ་པའི་སྐྲབས་སུ

རུ་ཚང་སྐྱོད་ཆེ་ན་འཐུལ་འཐུམས་སུ་འགྲོ་ཉིན་ཆེ་བས་རྡུན་རྗེ་མི་བརྟེད་པར་བརྟེན་
དགོས། གནས་འགྱུ་རིག་གསུམ་གང་གི་སྐྲབས་སུ་འང་རིག་མཁན་གྱི་རིག་
པ་སོ་མའི་ངང་དུ་ཅེར་གྱིས་བལྟས་ཏེ་སྐྱོམ་པ་གནད་གལ་ཆེའོ། །དེ་ལྟར་སྐྱོམ་
པའི་སྐྲབས་སུ་རིག་པ་ལྡིང་བའི་ཧྲགས་སུ་རྣམ་རྟོག་འཕྲོ་ཀྲོད་དང་ཉིན་མོངས་
པའི་རྟོག་ཚོགས་སྤྱར་བས་མང་བ་སྐྱམ་པ་དང་། བདེ་གསལ་མི་རྟོག་པ་ལ་
སོགས་པའི་ཉམས་ཀྱི་འཆར་སྒོ་མཐའ་ཡས་པ་ཞིག་འཆར་བས་དེ་དག་གང་
ལའང་རེ་དོགས་དགའ་སྐྱུག་ཞེན་འཛིན་མི་བྱ་བར་ཕར་མཁན་གྱི་རིག་པ་ལ་ཅེར་
གྱིས་བལྟས་ལ་བསྒོམ་པས་དེ་དག་གྲོགས་སུ་འཆར་བ་ཡིན། ཞེན་འཛིན་བྱུང་
ན་འཆིང་བར་གྱུར་རོ། ཁྱེས་པ་ད་ཅང་བྱིང་རྨུག་ཏུ་འགྱུར་ཏེ་རིག་པའི་
གསལ་ཆ་མ་ཐོན་ན་སྐྱིང་ཁར་ཨཝང་འོད་ཀྱི་གོང་བུ་བསྒོམས་ལ་དེ་ཉིད་སྤྱི་བོ་
ནས་རྒྱངས་ཀྱིས་ཐོན་ཏེ་མདའ་གང་ཙམ་གྱི་ནམ་མཁར་ལྡིང་སྐྲབས་སུ་གནས་
པར་སྐྱོམ་ལ་ཌུང་ཕྱིར་བཟུང་བས་སེལ་ལོ། །རུ་ཚང་ཉོད་ཆེས་ན་ལུས་སེམས་
ཁོང་སྐྱོད་ལྷུ་སྱངས་སྐྱད། སྐུ་ཅེར་ཐིག་ལེ་སྐྱོམ་པས་སེལ་ལོ། །གཞན་
ཡང་སྐྲབས་འགག་སྤྱིན་མེད་པའི་ནམ་མཁའ་དྲངས་པའི་ཚེ་ཉི་མ་ལ་རྒྱབ་བསྟན་
ནས་མིག་ནམ་མཁའི་དཀྱིལ་དུ་གཏད་ཅིང་རྦུང་རབ་ཏུ་དལ་བ་ཕྱིར་བཟུང་བས་
སྐྱད་ཅིག་ལ་རིག་སྟོང་ཟང་ཐལ་རྗེན་པའི་ཚོས་སྐྱ་ཁོང་ནས་འཆར་བ་ནི་ནམ་
མཁའ་སུམ་ཕྲུག་གི་དགོངས་པ་ཞེས་མཚོག་ཏུ་ཟབ་པའི་མན་ངག་གོ །ཡང་
ལུས་ཆོས་བདུན། རྐང་རང་བབས། སེམས་རྟོག་མེད་དུ་ཌར་ཅིག་བཞག
ཟེས། ཀང་ལག་བརྒྱང་སྟེ་གན་རྒྱལ་དུ་ཉལ་ནས་མིག་ནམ་མཁར་
གཏད། རུ་དྲག་པོ་གསུམ་བརྗོད་ལ་རྦུང་ཕྱིར་བཏང་སྟེ་སེམས་རང་སོར་
བཞག་པས་རྟོག་ཐུལ་ཆོས་ཉིད་ཀྱི་དགོངས་པ་འཆར་བ་ཡིན་ནོ། །ཡང་ལུས་
གནད་ཆོས་བདུན་སོགས་སྔར་ལྟར་རང་བབས་སུ་བཞག་པའི་ཚེ་གང་སྐྱང་ཡང་
སྐྱང་ཐོག་ཏུ་མི་བཞག་པར་སྐྱོང་ཐོག་གི་སྟེང་ཕྱི་ནང་བར་མེད་ཉར་སངས་སུ་ཐུབ

ནེ་ཤིག་གི་ལྷ་སྲུངས་བཅུན་ནས་བཞག་པས་སྐྱོང་བ་ནམ་མཁའ་ལྟ་བུའི་རྟོགས་པ་
འཆར་རོ། །ཡང་སྐྱོང་ཐོག་ཏུ་མི་བཞག་པར་སྲུང་བ་རང་གསལ་འཛིན་མེད་
ཀྱི་ངང་དུ་བཞག་པས་སྲུང་བ་འཛིན་མེད་ཁྲོལ་ཁྲོལ་གྱིས་རྟོགས་པ་འཆར་
རོ། །ཡང་རིག་པ་དྲངས་ནས་འཕོ་འདུའི་རྟོག་པ་འཆར་བ་ལ་གཏད་
པས། རྟེན་མེད་འཛིན་མེད་དུ་གྲོལ་བ་ར་རྣབས་ཆུར་ཐིམ་པ་ལྟ་བུའི་རྟོགས་པ་
འཆར་རོ། །འདི་དག་ནི་ཉམས་བཅོན་ཐབས་སུ་སྐྱེ་བས་ངེས་ཤེས་རྒྱུད་ལ་
སྐྱེད་པའི་ཐབས་ཟབ་མོའོ། །མཐར་ན་སྤྱར་སྒོས་པའི་རིག་པ་རང་གནས་ཀྱི་
བསམ་གཏན་ཀ་དག་ཆོས་ཟད་ཀྱི་དགོངས་པ། དགེ་སྡིག་སྐྱོན་ཡོན་ལས་
འདས་པ། གྲུབ་གསལ་འཕོ་འགྱུར་དང་བྲལ་བ། གཟུང་འཛིན་བློ་འདས་
ཀྱི་ཡེ་ཤེས། དབུ་ཕྱུག་རྟོགས་གསུམ་ཀྱི་དགོངས་པའི་སྒྱུལ་སོ་མཐར་ཕྱག་པ་
དེ་ཉིད་དུས་ཐམས་ཅད་དུ་ཡོད་པས་ཏེ་ཤེས་པར་བྱས་ཏེ་དེའི་དང་དུ་ཆེད་དུ་རྩོལ་
བས་མ་སྦྱིམ་ཡེངས་པས་ཕྱལ་བར་མ་སོང་བར་རང་བབས་མ་བཅོས་རྒྱ་པོའི་
རྒྱུན་གྱི་རྣལ་འབྱོར་སྐྱོང་བ་ལ་ཉམས་ལེན་གྱི་སྐྱིང་པོ་འདུག་བ་ཡིན། དེའི་
སྐབས་སུ་ཚོགས་དྲུག་གི་ཤེས་པ། དུག་ལྔའི་རྟོག་ཚོགས། ཉམས་ཀྱི་
འཕེལ་འགྲིབ་གང་དང་ཅི་ཤར་ཡང་ནམ་མཁའ་ལ་འཇའ་ཚོན་རྣམ་རྒྱ་ལ་ཐ་
རྣབས་བཞིན་རིག་པ་བྱུང་རྒྱབ་སེམས་ཀྱི་རྩལ་ལས་རོལ་པར་ཤར་བ་སྟེ་སྲུང་ན་
སྲུང་བར་མ་ཉམས། སྐྱོང་ན་སྐྱོང་པར་མ་ཉམས། བདེན་ན་བདེན་པར་
མ་ཉམས། ཐུན་ན་ཐུན་པར་མ་ཉམས། ཐམས་ཅད་རིག་པའི་ཚོ་འཕྱུལ་ལས་
གཞན་མེད་པས་དགག་སྒྲུབ་བླང་དོར་སྲུང་གཉེན་ཞེན་འཛིན་གང་ཡང་མི་བྱུ་བར་
ཤར་མཁན་གྱི་རིག་པ་སོ་མའི་ངང་དུ་ཕྱམ་གདལ་འཛིན་མེད་དུ་སྐྱོང་པས་གང་
ཤར་རང་གྲོལ་རྟོགས་པའི་རྩལ་སྐྱང་བར་གཅེས་སོ། །འདིའི་ཚེ་གནས་པའི་ཆ་
ནས་ཞི་གནས་དང་། རིག་སྐྱོང་ཟང་ཐལ་རྗེན་པར་རྟོགས་པའི་ཆ་ནས་ལྷག་
མཐོང་ཞེས་བཏགས་ཀྱང་དོན་སོ་སོར་འབྱེར་མེད་དོ། །རིག་པའི་ངོ་བོ་སྐྱོང་

པར་རྟོགས་པས་རྟག་པའི་མཐའ་ལས་གྲོལ། རང་བཞིན་གསལ་བར་མཐོང་
བས་ཆད་པའི་མཐའ་ལས་གྲོལ། བདེ་གསལ་མི་རྟོག་པའི་ཉམས་ལ་སྒོམ་དུ་
མི་རེ་བས་ཁམས་གསུམ་གྱི་ས་ལས་གྲོལ། གཉེན་པོའི་འཛིན་སྡངས་ཞིག
པས་གོལ་གྱིབ་གཞིས་ལ་མི་གནས། བློས་བྱས་ཡིད་དཔྱོད་ཀྱི་གཟེབ་ནས་
བྱང་ཆུབ་སྱི་དུས་ལ་མི་རེ་བར་ད་ལྟ་ཉིད་ནས་སྐུ་གསུམ་རང་ཆས་སུ་གནས་པ
ཉིད་ལམ་དུ་བྱེད་པ་འདི་རྟོགས་པ་ཆེན་པོའི་ཁྱད་པར་གྱི་ཆོས་སོ། །དེ་ལྟར་
རྟོགས་པའི་རྣལ་འབྱོར་པ་ཅི་ལྟར་གནས་ཀྱང་བློ་བདེ་བའི་ཉི་མ་ཁོང་ནས་འཆར་
བ་ལགས་སོ། །ཀོགས་དང་གོལ་ས་ཐམས་ཅད་རེ་རོགས་བདེན་ཞེན་འཛིན་པ
ལས་བྱུང་བས་གང་ལའང་མི་འཛིན་པ་གལ་ཆེའོ། །ལུས་ལ་ན་
ཚ། སེམས་ལ་སྡུག་བསྔལ། ཉེན་མོངས་ཞེན་འཛིན་དགག་སྒྲུབ་རང་
མཚན་པ་གང་དང་ཅི་ཤར་ཡང་དེ་ཉིད་རོས་བཟུང་ལ་བླ་མའི་གསོལ་འདེབས་བྱིན་
ཕེབས་པ་གཅིག་བྱས་ཏེ། དགག་སྒྲུབ་ཀྱི་ཤེས་པ་དེ་གང་ནས་བྱུང་གང་ན
གནས་གང་དུ་སོང་སོགས་གོ་སྟུ་ཚམ་དུ་མ་སོང་བར་ཞིབ་ཏུ་བརྟགས་ཤིང་བཙལ
ན་གང་དུའང་མ་གྲུབ་ཅེ་ལའང་མི་གནས། འདི་ཞེས་ཚིག་གིས་མི་མཚོན་པའི་
གཟུང་འཛིན་བློ་འདས་ཀྱི་ཡེ་ཤེས་རིག་སྟོང་རྗེན་པའི་ཆོས་སྐུ་ཁོང་ནས་མི་འཆར་
བ་མི་སྲིད་པས། དེ་འཆར་བ་དང་དེ་ཁའི་རང་བསྐྱང་བས་གོགས་དང་གོལ་
ས་མཐའ་དག་རང་གྲོལ་དུ་འགྲོ་བ་ཡིན་ནོ། །ཁོགས་འདོན་ཐམས་ཅད་ཀྱི
རྒྱལ་པོ་བླ་མའི་མོས་གུས་ཡིན་པས་ཐ་མལ་མི་རུ་བཟུང་བའི་བློ་སྤང་སྟེ་སངས་
རྒྱས་དངོས་སུ་མཐོང་བའི་དད་མོས་དང་མ་བྲལ་བ་གཅེས་སོ། །གཞན་ཡང
མི་རྟག་པ་དང་། སྙིང་རྗེ། བསྐྱེད་རིམ། རྫོགས་རིམ་མཚན་བཅས་
མཚན་མེད་རྣམས་སྒྲུལ་མར་བསྒོམ་ན། གཅིག་བོགས་གཅིག་གིས་ཐོན་ཏེ་ས
ཆེད་ཤིག་ཏུ་ཆེ་བ་ཡིན། སྔུན་རྗེས་སུ་བསྒོ་བ་དང་། སྔུན་མཚམས་སུའང
ཆོས་ཐམས་ཅད་སྒྱུ་མ་ལྟ་བུར་ལྟ་བའི་ལམ་ཁྱེར་དང་མ་བྲལ་བར་བྱ། མཚན

མོ་གཉིད་ཀྱི་རྣལ་འབྱོར་ཡང་རྒྱལ་ཁར་གཉིད་འོད་གསལ་དུ་འཁར་བར་གསོལ་
བ་གདབ་རྗེས་བླ་མ་དང་རང་སེམས་བསྲེས་ཏེ་རིག་པ་སོ་མའི་ངང་བསྐྱང་ལ་རྣམ་
རྟོག་གཞན་གྱིས་བར་མ་ཆོད་པར་གཉིད་དུ་འགྲོ་བར་བྱའོ། །གཞན་ཡང་ཉེས་
པར་བྱ་བའི་གནད་ནི་སྐྲ་བས་ལ་མ་རྨོས་ན་གཟུང་འཛིན་བདེན་ཞེན་གྱི་འཆིང་བ་མི་
ཞིག་པས་མཉམ་བཞག་གི་སྣང་བས་སུ་ཆོས་ཐམས་ཅད་མེད་ཕྱལ་ལྷུན་གྲུབ་གཅིག
པུར་ལ་བརྟག་བ་གཅེས་སོ། །སློབ་པའི་དང་མ་བསྐྱང་ན་ཡིན་པ་ཙམ་གྱིས་
གནད་ཐོག་ཏུ་མི་ཕེབས་པས་བཙོན་འགྲུས་རྒྱུན་བསྲིང་བ་གལ་ཆེའོ། །སྟོང་
པས་གནས་མ་འབྱེད་ན་དགོ་སྟོང་སྙིག་སྟོང་ནག་པོ་ཁ་འབྱམས་སུ་འགྲོ་ཉེན་ཆེ་བས་
རྟེས་ཐོབ་ཏུ་སྐྱ་མ་ལྤུ་བུ་དང་འགྲོགས་ནས་ལས་འབྲས་མི་བསྒྲུ་བའི་རེས་ཉེས་
བཏུན་པོས་ཆེ་བྱེད་དགོ་བའི་ལས་སུ་བསྒྱུར་བ་གནད་དོ། །ཐབས་ཤེས་ཡ་བྲལ་
དུ་གྱུར་ན་ནམ་ཡང་འཆིང་བས་སྟོང་ཉིད་དང་སྙིང་རྗེ། །བསོད་ནམས་དང་ཡེ་
ཤེས་ཀྱི་ཚོགས་གཉིས་ཟུང་དུ་འབྲེལ་བ་རྒྱལ་བ་དགྱེས་པའི་ལམ་བཟང་དུ་འཛུག་
པ་གལ་ཆེའོ། །འདི་དག་ནི་མཆོག་ཏུ་གཅེས་པའི་ཆེང་ས་གལ་པོ་ཆེ་ལགས་
པས་ཕུགས་ལ་དེ་བཞིན་བཞག་འཚལ། །མི་ཏྲ་སྲོ་ཤས་རྒྱུད་ལ་མ་སྐྱེས་
ན། །ལྷར་སྐྱང་ཆེ་འདི་སྒྲུབ་པའི་ཕྱེལ་དོ་ཡིས། །དམ་ཆོས་གཏན་མ་
འགྲུབ་དུས་མི་གདའ་བས། །བཙོས་མིན་དེས་འབྱུང་རྒྱུད་ལ་སྐྱེ་བར་
ཤོག །སྙིང་རྗེ་བྱང་ཆུབ་སེམས་མཆོག་མ་སྟོང་ན། །རང་དོན་ཡིད་བྱེད་
འཛིན་པའི་མུན་ཁྲོད་ནས། །ཐེག་ཆེན་ལམ་བཟང་སྣང་དུས་མི་གདའ་
བས། །ཡང་དག་བྱང་ཆུབ་སེམས་མཆོག་འབྱུར་བར་ཤོག །འཕགས་
པས་མ་ཐོབ་གཞན་དོན་ལྷུར་སྲུང་ཚ། །གཞན་ལ་མི་ཕན་རང་ཉིད་འཆིང་བའི་
རྒྱུ། །རྣམ་གཡེངས་འདུ་འཛིའི་མགོ་བོ་མི་འཁོར་བར། །དབེན་པའི་
གནས་སུ་སྒྲུབ་ལ་བརྟོན་པར་ཤོག །ཐབས་ཤེས་ཡ་བྲལ་སྐྱེས་བུ་ཀུན་ཆག
བཞིན། །རྣམ་མཁྱེན་ས་ལམ་བགྲོད་པའི་མཐུ་བྲང་པས། །སྟོང་ཉིད་སྙིང་རྗེ་

བསྐྱེད། རྟོགས་ཚོགས་གཉིས་པོ། །བྱང་འབྲེལ་མ་ནོར་ལམ་ལ་འཇུག །
པར་ཤོག །བརྒྱུད་ལྡན་བླ་མའི་བྱིན་རླབས་མ་འཕོས་ན། །སྤུག་བཙོར་
སྒོམ་པས་གནས་ལུགས་མི་རྟོགས་པས། །མོས་གུས་ཆེད་དུ་གྱུར་པའི་རྟེན་
འབྲེལ་གྱིས། །དགོངས་བརྒྱུད་འཕོ་བའི་དབང་མཆོག་ཐོབ་པར་ཤོག །
རང་རིག་འོད་གསལ་བློ་འདས་རྟོགས་པ་ཆེ། །སྐུ་དང་ཡེ་ཤེས་ཡེ་ནས་ལྷུན་
གྲུབ་པས། །ཡིན་ལུགས་ཅིག་གཤག་བཞི་ཡི་མན་ངག་གིས། །བྲད་པའི་
ས་ལ་གཏན་སྲིད་ཟིན་པར་ཤོག །ནམ་ཞིག་འགྲོ་ལ་ཕན་པའི་གནས་ཐོབ་
ཆེ། །གཞན་དོན་མི་སློ་བཟོད་པའི་གོ་བགོས་ཏེ། །མཁའ་མཉམ་མ་རྣམས་
སྲིད་པའི་རྒྱ་པོ་ལས། །བདག་ཉིད་གཅིག་པུས་ཡོངས་སུ་བསྒྲལ་གྱུར་
ཅིག །རྣལ་འབྱོར་པ་ཡན་པ་བློ་བདེས་བྱོགས་པོ་ཀ་མ་ཡིའི་མིང་ཅན་ལ་
གདམས་པ་ལས་དང་པོ་པ་ལ་སྨན་པའི་ཉུ་པ་དེ་ཤའོ། །རེ་ཞིག་རྟོགས་
སོ། །ཀྱཻ༔༔

INDEX